PURPLE The Courageous Little Elephant

By
Arlene Hernandez

DEDICATION

To my nephew Mario Christopher Aguirre, Mexican Boy. When children listen to stories, it leaves them with a humongous impression on their developing minds, and their little blessed hearts. When the story projects enthusiasm and warmth, it sticks to the soul. Somewhere in time, many of those stories become part of their own heritage, legends. Life is wonderful knowing that my nephew still recalls my silly, out-of-this-world made up stories. I hope that one day, he will share them with his own children.

Let me tell you an adorable story about a little elephant that wasn't as small as everyone had figured. His name was Purple. He struggled for many years to be accepted for who he truly was: a BIG boy. Because of his wee-size body, his parents treated him like a baby cub all his life. If he could only muster up the courage to show them, but most of all, to show himself, that despite his minuscule size, he was all grown up inside.

The story goes like this: Somewhere deep in the African continent, by a remote savanna timberland, on the other side of Congo, lived a large-eared family of elephants. There were many of them in that pride. There were brothers and sisters. Cousins, aunts, and uncles. Parents and grandparents, and even great-grandparents. Well, you know, the BIG ones, the middle-sized ones, and the itty-bitty ones. The latter critters were so darn cute. Indeed, they were.

Purple, the perpetual runt, along with all the other little ones, loved to play tag every time they could. Their happy roaring filled the air with joy. But every good thing must end or come to a pause. Soon, you could hear a thunderous sound as they crashed into each other like a pile of rocks. Then, they would take a quick nap. After a minute of snoozes, they would get up on all fours, race down to the water pools, and gulp down gallons of murky water. How refreshing! At the pools, they would play calf games, like Marco Polo. Yup. They enjoyed that game as well. Who doesn't? After a good rinse-off, back to the boulders!

Like lightning, they sped to the boulders at a smooth pace of 15mph. Nowhere near a cheetah, but hey, they could easily outrun a house mouse. Anyhow, with stretched out trunks, the winner got the prize. What prize? _____ That inner feeling of satisfaction. Oh Yeah! Then, they would all gallantly scuffle toward the white picket fence that no one ever dared to cross. Wait. What? And why wouldn't they cross it?

It's because there was an old wives' tale told and retold about that little white picket fence. It was a legend amongst the elephant kingdoms. The eldest female, with droopy eyes, reminded the little ones just how dangerous it was on the other side of the little white picket fence. Really? Everyone believed the story. Would you? _____ Well, one part of the fable that impressed the little critters the most was the part about the four tree trunks. Hmm. This is how the tale went:

"Set your eyes upon those four tree trunks way out there to the right. Do you see them, my dear young ones? If you look closely enough, you'll notice that they don't have branches, or any delicious leaves to eat. Compared to the other trees, they're just dried up stumps. Do they not remind you of something? To me, they look like the legs of your Babu Kubwa (great grandfather)."

After an exhausted sigh, she continued:

If my memory serves me right, a loooong time ago, a little elephant about your size Purple, wandered off to explore the wilderness all by himself. Maybe, he saw something interesting that tickled him pink, and he became daring enough to veer off on his own. (Back then, there was no fence.) Whatever the case, he must have been a waasi (rebel). His parents constantly trump-called that little rascal. But after many deliberate escapes, one day, he didn't return to the herd. For days, months, and years, the family looked and looked for him with no success. Eventually, they gave up. I remember being on that utafutail na vokoaji (search and rescue posse). Great Grandpa had us make one more desperate distinct trumpet call at the top of our trunks that sounded like a roaring army ready to ascend onto the battlefield. Still nothing."

After fluttering her lashes, she continued:

"One springtime, when we returned to our nyumbani (homeland), after the long winter break, we found four tree trunks close to one another. As I said earlier, they had no branches, nor did they give any chakula (food). There were just four posts in a hole. Watu (people) came and went. Some would stay for a time, while others would move on after a season or two. They made little huts near the four tree trunks. Some used them to hang up their skins. Other settlers would build swings for their young. Either way, they put the posts to good use."

Now, back to the crux of the story.

Just a little wee elephant's tail could have knocked down that whole fence in a jiffy. For goodness' sake, someone made it out of wood planks and a thin layer of white paint—a picket fence, to be exact. But something about those resilient pickets caused even the bravest elephant to tremble at the slightest chance of touching it. That's just the way it was. The powerful tale of the picket fence followed every new generation with the slightest variation.

When the new calves appeared on the scene, they would go out and play with Purple. Well, let's just say, they learned quickly when to put on the brakes. After tagging the boulders and then racing off with unbelievable momentum, they'd leave everything in the dust. And all living creatures on that path would move to the side and let them pass or else. Yet, a little white picket fence forever stopped them on their tiptoes. Yes, they have toes.

Believe me, they'd get up mighty close to the fence, but never super close. The sudden halt kicked up loosened dirt and rubble that flung toward the fence, which caused more white paint to chip off the uzio wa mbao (picket fence). Some of those pebbles even crossed over to the other side and would land on the soft, undisturbed blanket of wild grass. Not that anyone noticed.

Except for one little purple runt out of the bunch of calves that noticed just about everything. This little thing didn't look much different from the others. And if it's true, that elephants can't see certain colors, then no one should ever have thought anything was wrong with him. But you and I can see that it was different, right? ______

The little purple elephant knew how to live it up, and the reason was that he played with several other generations of little elephants over a long period of time. He knew his territory very well. At one time or later, all those little calves grew up, yet Purple stayed smallish, like forever.

Every generation of calves poked fun at Purple as they themselves began to grow tusks and would pass him up, in height and stature. They would grow out of the playful mood, too. They also learned to do grown-up stuff like butt heads with other elephants, knock down trees, breed, and take the lead in their own families.

Purple never had the chance to do those things. His parents would always send him off to play with the 'NEW KIDS' on the block. "Now, go ahead and play with your little friends." Mama would say. But Purple didn't want to play all the time. He wanted to experience BIG elephant stuff.

That's why during one early spring, he strolled off by himself, within the elephant kingdom boundaries. He made sure he wouldn't end up like the four tree trunks. He started looking for other smaller life forms to boss them around because he wanted to feel BIG.

That morning, he walked himself to the end of the white picket fence. Out of nowhere, he bumped into a stinky warthog. It was smaller than Purple. So, Purple imagined he could rule him for a spell. After exchanging sniffs and mean looks at each other, they both realized that friendship was the only solution.

Every early morning thereafter, Purple downed his meal, and no sooner did his mom shove him off to play. He'd go meet up with Puggy, but Puggy didn't live by the white picket fence law. Sometimes, as they would stroll along one end of the fence to the other end, Purple would walk on this side, while Puggy pressed his hooves on the soft blanket of undisturbed grass on the other side.

They had a couple of adventurous moments together, like the time when they took on a conglomerate of kidogo aardvarks. After the sunset, and the trees cast a deep shadow over there, Puggy and Purple tiptoed from boulder to boulder until they were close enough to take command of the situation.

As the six-month-old aardvarks ventured out of their pit in search of grub, the duo rolled a small boulder over it. A shadowy fear soon came upon the aardvarks. First, they attempted to zoom back into their den, but immediately realized something was covering the hole with a rock. There was nothing else they could do but to stand at a switcheroo and face their demise.

Now, the interrogation began: "What brings you little critters out at night? Isn't it your bedtime?" Puggy gave out a snort and then continued the bullying. "Hey! I am talking to you, squirts. Did you forget your manners?"

They both busted in laughter.

"Why the long face?" Puggy added, with a perplexed look.

They began to turn around simultaneously. To their surprise, they, too, had snouts at the tips of their long trunks. Soon, the duo realized that they might be cousins of a sort.

"What you guys called?" asked Purple.

One of them took a deep swallow and said with a dry voice, "the natives call us earth pigs. We come out at night to eat our breakfast, lunch, and dinner."

Purple replied, "You wanna play with us? We promise we will not hurt you. We can walk on our tiptoes. See?"

Purple and Puggy both started dancing like sissies. The aardvarks burst out in laughter and joined them in song and dance. They had a wonderful time together that evening before the two had to head back home. On their way back, Purple flicked the boulder off the pit. And they both skippididood back home.

Puggy eventually grew tusks because he was turning into an adult and so he abandoned Purple to build his own family. Every so often, Purple looked to the area where he himself should grow tusks. All he would see was soft fur that needed a cut.

One lonely day, Purple took the two-mile stroll along the white picket fence all by his lonesome. Somehow, his dejected trunk flopped right over the fence. His little trunk-tip softly brushed over the undisturbed grass shoots. It felt so good; better yet, nothing bad happened.

As he continued strolling along, he met up with a group of little elephants poised two feet from the fence. He heard them whispering something. As he got close enough to ask them what they were talking about, Tank, the buffed one, spoke: "Hey, Purple. What ya doin? Wanna play truth or dare?"

"Sure, why not?" he answered.

"Ok. Which will it be, truth or dare?" he asked Purple.

"I guess the truth," Purple replied with perky ears.

"Say, why are you so little? Aren't you like 100 years old? And why haven't your tusks poked out?"

Purple was instantly humiliated. His perky ears fell to the ground, and his trunk followed. "I change my mind. I'll pick dare."

"Ok!" Tank turned his head and winked at the others.

"Tell him to jump over the fence." They whispered.

Tank raised his ears high and mighty like his grandpa did. Then he ordered Purple, "Jump the fence. Do it now!"

Purple froze. Not even his tail swayed a bit.

The bunch of little elephants burst out in laughter and ran off, saying, "Clack, clack, clack, clack…"

Poor Purple. He simply did not fit in with the other elephants.

One early spring, when he came out to stroll, he caught sight of something strange over there by the white picket fence. Why, it was hopping over the fence, back and forth. Purple stared in amazement. He even moved closer to the little strange object and found it was a little pink ball bouncing back and forth. He kept following it with his eyes like a furious tennis match until his ears wound around his head.

After unwrapping himself, he took 20 giant steps back, and the little ball followed him. Whenever Purple would stop, so would the ball. When he got close to it, the ball would retreat. This continued like forever.

That evening, Purple told his parents about what he had discovered, but they didn't believe his tale.

Right away, his father spoke up: "It's time for you to start a family of your own because we are now ancient and can't care for calves anymore."

Purple was the last one living with them, obviously.

And he knew well. In fact, he was all grown up inside even though his body was still half-pint size. So, he set off to begin a thorough search for a suitable wife. That is, on this side of the picket fence, of course. But the medium-sized ones and the giant-sized elephants would shove him toward the calves to play.

AAAH!

That evening, as the sun had not quite set on the boulders, he walked toward the white picket fence. He was hoping to meet up again with the little pink ball, and he did. It was waiting for him perched on the fence right on a picket, like a golf tee.

The ball excitedly jumped off and landed on this side of the fence. It stood right next to Purple's foot. Then, with a sudden pounce, it met him eye-to-eye. Purple stared right back into the ball. He had nothing to lose.

Inside the mystery ball, he saw purple clouds. Softly, he blew into it and the clouds opened and over there in the far distance stood acres and acres of purple grass.

All around were elephants that looked like Purple, little happy elephants. Awe! That seemed right for Purple. It all began to make sense to him. That's where he could start a family.

But how was all that going to be possible when Purple was so BIG and the ball so tiny? Well, the ball backed up cautiously and zoomed over the fence as if it was waving Purple to follow it.

Purple had rules, as we are all aware of. Rules that he lived by for a long, long time. *'NEVER cross the white picketed fence.'* At first Purple acquiesced to the ancient rule and slowly turned away and began walking back to the herd feeling disappointed in himself.

But then something happened to his head. It was like a little light was triggered in his noggin. He stopped acting like a frightened cat. With determination, he perked up his ears, spun around, and charged the fence with all his might. 20 feet, 10 feet, 5 feet, 2 feet, 1 foot and 0 inches. When he reached the top of the picket fence, he stopped. Blah.

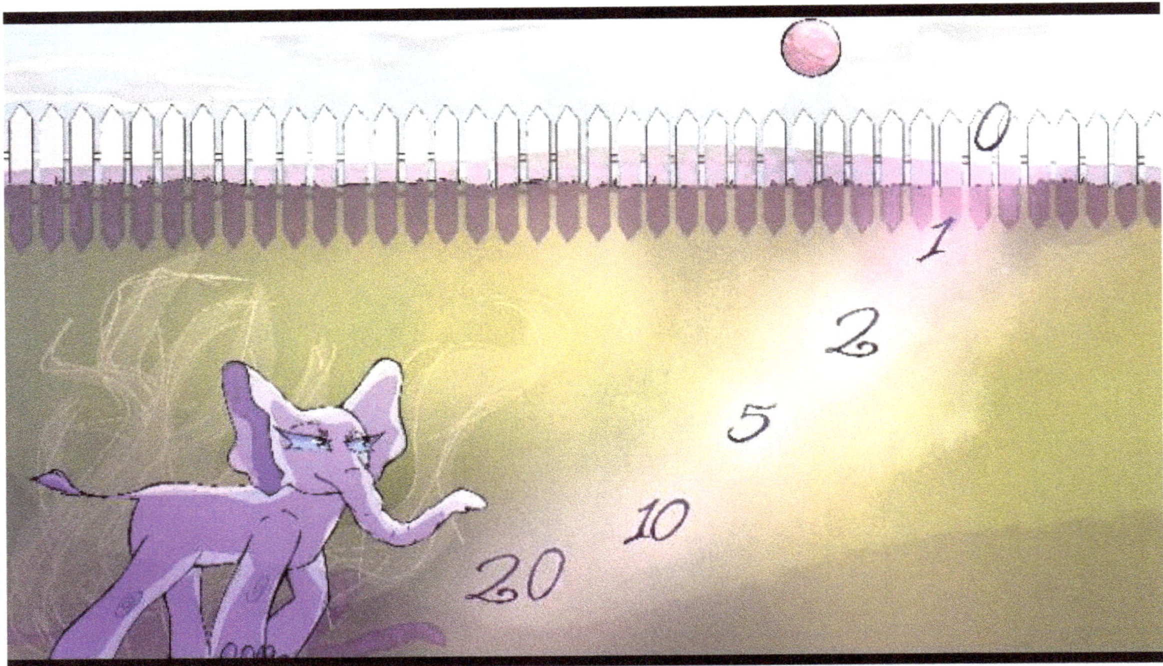

His round little body teetered and tottered several times. As he teetered closer to the other side, his ears feathered the undisturbed tips of the long green shoots. Then he tottered back and let himself fall on his side. He couldn't do it. He kept hearing the voice of the old wise elephant with the droopiest eyelids saying, *"DO NOT CROSS OVER!"* Purple sat flat on his bottom. The little pink ball patiently waited back on the picket.

After a long wait, (because he was thinking for a long time), Purple raised up his head, shook off the vijiba, (jibbers), took 20 giant steps back, and then, with all his powers, once again charged the fence! Purple looked so brave and BIG and strong like a grownup. The lad charged 20 feet, 10 feet, 5 feet, 2 feet, then one foot. He leaped his whole body over the fence.

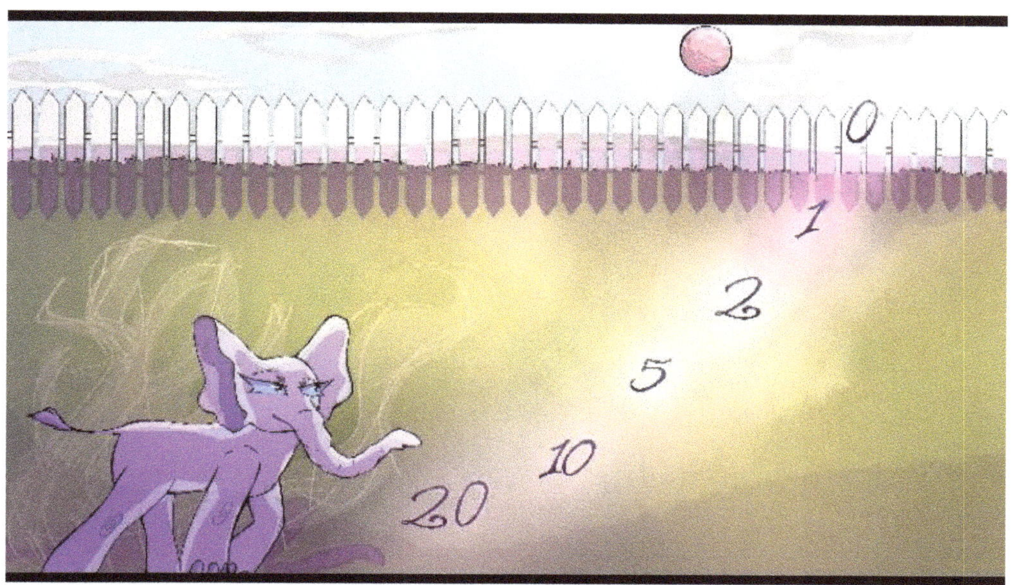

The back of his feet kicked off, and he broke the fence, and he shot up so high into the air like a rocket. In the blink of an eye, Purple started shrinking as he headed toward the little pink ball. Yikes! The ball enveloped him within seconds.

Before long, Purple landed on the soft purple grass, followed by a few tumbles. Then he stood up, a little embarrassed. Wouldn't you if you fell on your rump? Surrounding him were tons of purple elephants, all cheering and welcoming him.

The little purple elephant finally made a family of his very own. And guess what? ____ He was the BIGGEST one of them all.

SUMMARY

We all live with some type of boundaries, either enforced by parents or by the law of the land. That's fair. But should some laws become unlearned if it impedes us from true happiness? Purple had laws he abided by, but at some point, his ancient parents released him from their law. Purple took leaping strides after several generations of the same old life. Let's see where it got him.

Moral: The power of determination vs cowardice.

Word Translation Chart

English	Swahili
Great Grandfather	Babu Mkubwa
Rebel	Waasi
Search and Rescue Posse	Utafutaji na uokoaji posse
Homeland	Nyumbani
Food	Chakula
People	Watu
Dear Young Ones	Wapendwa Vijana
Branches	Matawi
Little Elephant	Tembo Mdogo